wild horses
in the Namib Desert

 *here i am, wild and free*

An equine biography

Mannfred Goldbeck & Telané Greyling
As told to Ron Swilling

Honouring the spirit of the horse

Published by Friends of the Wild Horses
© Copyright Mannfred Goldbeck and Telané Greyling

No part of this book may be reproduced or transmitted in any form or by any means, electronic or mechanical, including photocopying, recording, or by any information storage or retrieval system, without the written permission of the authors
telanie@namibhorses.com • md@gondwana-collection.com • ronswilling@gmail.com
www.wild-horses-namibia.com

Printed by John Meinert Printing, Windhoek, 2011
ISBN: 978-99945-72-52-6

Layout & Design
Heike Lorck

contents

Foreword

Here I Am, Wild and Free Again …

1
Return to Freedom
Page 11

2
The Past:
Page 21
The Arrival of Horses in the Namib Desert
The Summer of 1915 in Garub
A step into the imagination/Origin Theories
In the Safety of the Sperrgebiet: 1920-1977

3
A Changing of Perception:
Page 43
1977 to the present time
Research and Reality: Clearing doubts and planning for the future
Embodying the spirit of Namibia

4
Wild Horse Behaviour
Page 57
The essentials
Social structure
It's not black and white
Body language
Risks, threats and survival
The lean and the fat years
Sex ratio, breeding success and the gene pool
Adaptations to the Namib Desert

The Dream
Page 86

Appendix
The Challenge: Finding the balance between the norm and the natural

Acknowledgements

References

'There's something about the outside of a horse
that is good for the inside of a man.'

Winston Churchill

foreword

The concept for the book **Wild Horses in the Namib Desert** has been incubating for many years in the hearts and minds of Mannfred Goldbeck and Telané Greyling who share an interest and passion for these animals.

Steeped in mystery, there has been much speculation as to the horses' origins. The book seeks to clarify the origins of the wild horse population living in the Namib Desert as well as to enlighten readers about their behaviour and more recent history, while answering the innumerable questions that are continually asked about these intriguing creatures.

The historical research, essential in shedding light on the mysterious origins of the horses, was undertaken by Mannfred Goldbeck who researched and identified the more plausible theories relating to the events that initiated the Garub wild horse population.

With more clarity cast on their beginnings, the understanding of the nature and behaviour of the Garub horses stemmed from Telané Greyling's (PhD Zoology) many years of field research and resulting doctoral thesis. She has monitored the horses for a period of sixteen years and presently acts in an advisory capacity to the Namibian Ministry of Environment and Tourism.

Freelance writer, Ron Swilling, created a text from the material giving it a breath of life.

Finally, from the love for the horse and all things wild, the book was born.

here i am, wild and free again . . .

'This is me …
There's nowhere else on Earth I'd rather be.'
It's a new day.

A scattering of stones extends into an expansive desert landscape of gravel plains streaked with short yellow grass tufts, dotted with clumps of hardy blue-green shrubs and edged with inselbergs and purple-blue mountains.

The soft golds and pinks of the dawn clear to bleached yellow as the summer sun rises and begins its onslaught onto the morning land. Jackal calls sound through the air and then recede with the darkness of the retreating night. We are one of the first groups of horses to arrive at the Garub water troughs as the day focuses into its crisp contours. I drink with my mares and foals and then we move off to the side as other horse groups appear in the distance, trotting in with sand clouds rising from their hooves – manes and tails flying, youngsters bucking and kicking, or walking in sedately to the troughs.

We move in a wave, an organic flow, a continuum of those arriving and disappearing over the horizon. Horses whinny, roll in the sand encircled by dust haloes and streaked with the ephemeral morning light, lie on the ground or stand statue-like under the merciless sun. Oryx with their sceptre-like horns approach the water troughs to drink, a springbok delicately makes its way on the rocky soil, Namaqua sandgrouse fly over and call in their distinctive lilting cadence and pied crows perch menacingly on the roof of the viewing hide waiting for opportune moments.

The blue of the sky has already set the colours for the day when a trail of dust heralds the arrival of a tourist vehicle to the viewpoint. My black mane is hot against my neck and the warmth of the day is spreading its fiery tendrils up through the ground. A family alights from the vehicle and takes cover in the shade of the hide, unaccustomed to the harshness of the Namibian climate. They admire our wild beauty, our bay and chestnut colours, shining as if burnished by the sun. Looking around at the seemingly barren land before them and feeling the heaviness of the day already beginning to burn, they wonder aloud if there is sufficient food for us to eat.

I listen to the strange bubbling words of the people as I look out onto the gravel plains and my home, the Namib Desert. We have adapted over a period of a hundred years from the time of our domesticated ancestors to this terrain that appears unforgiving yet offers us life and a home. We have formed family groups and bonds as Equus groups naturally do. There is an adequate supply of food. The dry years come in cycles, regulating our numbers. This is what we Namib horses know. This is who we are. We have no knowledge of fences and stables and the ways of man, or the lonely life away from our family groups. We know the summer heat, the winter cold, the powerful easterly winds that blow unwaveringly through the plains. We are accustomed to the oryx and ostrich, wary of the hyaena, and we know the grasses to eat and the place of water. We are at home, wild and free, under the blue African sky and scintillating stars of the Namib Desert.

CHAPTER 1

return to freedom

'As long as we do not ask the horse to forget who he is, he will remind us of who we want to be.'

Melissa Sovey-Nelson - 'If I Had a Horse'

Wild Horses. The words conjure up a host of strong images and bear a vast array of romantic notions: Horses running free in an expansive landscape whipping up dust, manes flying in the wind; muscular stallions rearing proudly; and the pounding of hooves as a group of wild horses thunders past with breathtaking energy and power. The wild horse populations around the world evoke feelings of freedom that touch us in the unfathomable depths of our being. They inspire our imagination and feed our spirit. The advertising and film industries use this powerful imagery, often depicting horses in vast landscapes, adding to the images which we already harbour.

Horses have been domesticated since ancient times, reined, harnessed and have served us loyally at the cost of their natural lives, changing the face of history and opening the world up to transport, travel and speed. Yet, their wild beauty still stirs us deeply whenever we have the chance to glimpse one of these rare populations. We empathise with domesticated horses' vanished freedom as we see their destiny mirrored in our structured lives in the confines of modern society. The existence of wild horses symbolises everything we have lost and which we long for in our personal lives. Whether we are horse lovers or not, they represent for us a deep longing to abandon our expected social norms and responsibilities, embrace free will and freedom, and to live untamed, unfettered lives.

Domesticated horses have not only lost their freedom and been exploited for millennia but they have lost their chance to form natural family units and bonds, and as such remain beautiful but dislocated beasts. In contrast, wild horses have reverted back to their wildness and natural ways with mares and stallions uniting and rearing foals in natural family groups with all the dynamics of wild Equidae. The paradox of human history is that humankind has been on a quest to tame, domesticate, exploit and control the world, yet when animals are encountered that have reclaimed their untamed nature, they settle in the human heart and stir the soul.

The Wild Horses in the Namib Desert have an added appeal, the allure of myth and mystery, and the embodiment of survival in an unforgiving landscape. At the turbulent time of World War I domesticated horses were abandoned in the arid regions of the Namib Desert as a result of the pursuits of men and absolute chance. Using their innate natural ability to survive, they endured and adapted over approximately a century to a harsh environment that over the years became home, forming a unique population. Like the majority of the Namibian population whose ancestors travelled from East and Central Africa and settled in the desert land, or arrived on ships from other continents and made the south-west African soil their home, the horses found themselves in a new land and over a period of seven generations adapted to the conditions

The 'zonkey', resulting from occasional cross-breeding of zebra and donkey, is evidence of their common equine ancestry.

Similarly, the 'zorse', a cross-breed between a horse and a zebra...

of this corner of Africa. Their history is inextricably woven into the history and development of the country, the emergence of new settlements, transport, the construction of railway lines, the chaos of local and foreign wars, the diamond rush, drought, growth and peace.

Moving even further back in time, the evolution of Equidae can be traced back to pre-history, about 52 million years ago, to an animal referred to as 'the Dawn Horse' or Eohippus (Hyracotherium), a small animal no larger than a dog. It is assumed that it lived in a jungle-like environment and was a browsing animal. Its four toes on the forefeet, three on the hind, terminating in thick horn and a foot pad would have given it greater mobility on soft soil in its forest surroundings. Further adaptations and developments in size, conformation, teeth and toes, probably in conjunction with changing climate, terrain and vegetation, enabled even greater mobility and variation in diet, culminating approximately four to eight million years ago in the prototype for the genus *Equus* which includes horses, zebras and asses (donkeys). *Equus caballus*, the 'true horse', became a long-legged agile creature of wide-open plains living in semi-arid regions, surviving on sparse vegetation where other large grazing animals, especially ruminants, could not. It remained wild until 5000-6000 years ago when nomadic peoples of the Eurasian steppes are said to have begun the process of domestication, changing its destiny forever.

During this vast time period of equine evolution, what we consider present day North America was linked by land bridges to Europe and Asia, as was Europe to Africa. Equidae migrated from North America over the land bridges to Asia, South America, Europe and finally North Africa. At the end of the ice age, when the land bridges disintegrated, four related forms of *Equus* remained in the Old World (Eurasia and Africa). They were the horses in Europe and western Asia, asses and zebras in the north and south of Africa respectively, and onagers (Asian wild asses) in the Middle East. The horse mysteriously became extinct in North America about 11 000 years ago, only to be reintroduced with the arrival of the Spanish conquistadores in the sixteenth century. The evolutionary branch comprising asses and zebras developed in the Old World and is distinguished by different physical characteristics. It is postulated that the evolution of the zebra involved the development of stripes as protection against predators, one of these being the dreaded and deadly tsetse fly from Central Africa, transmitter of 'sleeping sickness'. Tsetse flies are deterred by patterns or markings, preferring large plain-coloured subjects. This may be considered the reason why, unlike horses, zebras managed to gradually migrate southwards down the continent of Africa.

The domestic horse spread westward from Central Asia to Europe, and south into Arabia and China. For a period of 4000 years horses were essential for the advancement of civilisation. Man used them for war and conquest, agriculture and industry, and sport and recreation. They appear in artistic representations throughout mankind's history from Ancient Egyptian friezes to Greek vases, Roman reliefs to Chinese paintings. Modern horse breeds are the result of human intervention and selective breeding, resulting in numerous breeds developed for specific purposes and physical characteristics. There are over 300 breeds in the world today.

...and a mule, a cross-breed between a horse and a donkey. All the cross-bred progeny are unable to reproduce, except in rare cases.

The mule is a good example of hybrid vigour for the expression of beneficial characteristics of two species e.g. sure-footedness, strength and endurance. Humankind exploited this hardy mix to advance civilisation.

Horses were transported by ship and unloaded onto the coast of southern Africa

Pockets of wild horses exist on every continent on the planet, except for Antarctica, and on several islands. The Mongolian Wild Horse, also known as Przewalski's Horse, is the only horse never to have been domesticated and still existing in its true genetic form. Teetering on the brink of extinction, these horses known for their aggression and fierce temperament were considered extinct in the wild in the latter years of the twentieth century. However, a small breeding population that survived in captivity has since been reintroduced into its natural habitat. The Tarpan or Eurasian Wild Horse, once found in Europe and Asia, became extinct in 1918 when the last one died in a Ukrainian zoo. Other populations of wild horses are descended from domesticated ancestors and are often referred to as feral. These include the Mustangs of North America, the Brumbies of Australia, the Criollo of Argentina and the Sorraia of Spain. In South Africa there are a few small populations in the Drakensberg escarpment area in Mpumalanga, originating from the Gold Rush era, of which the Kaapsche Hoop and Morgenzon are the most well known. There is also a small group of wild horses living around the Bot River estuary near Hermanus in the Cape. Namibia is home to the Namib wild horses in the Namib Naukluft Park (with another small group at Aussenkehr in southern Namibia) and a separate, younger small population of wild horses in the Fish River Canyon.

Onto the southern tip of Africa

Horses only appeared in southern Africa in the seventeenth century 'when Holland was mistress of the seas'. The Cape of Good Hope served as a re-provisioning station from 1652 for the Dutch East India Company to supply the ships rounding the tip of Africa en route from Europe to the East. The first horses were requested by Jan van Riebeeck who was commissioned to establish the station, and who continually argued that his biggest hindrance was the shortage of horses. *'Horses are as necessary as bread in our mouths'*, he wrote. The horses which he received originated from South East Asia and had a strong Arabian-Persian influence, a small hardy breed familiar with drier climes. They were used as draught animals and for transport, field-work, protection,  hunting and exploration into the new colony. The price of one horse was equivalent to that of five to eight large oxen. Interestingly, in the first hundred years, only 42 horses were imported into the country. In the late 1700s several horses from South America, England and North America reached the Cape. Subsequent importations included horses of Oriental and Spanish blood. In the 1800s English Thoroughbreds and Hackneys were introduced, improving the bloodline of the tough, surefooted breed that had come to be referred to as the Cape Horse, *Afrikanische Pferd,* (later becoming known as the Boerperd) a fusion of the Javanese pony, Persians, English Thoroughbreds and Spanish Barbs. The Anglo-Boer War of 1899-1902 brought a large influx of horses to South Africa from Europe (mainly the United Kingdom), South America, Eastern Europe, Canada and Australia. It is told that of the 520 000 horses supplied to the English armed forces for the war, 350 000 perished. A horse memorial in Port Elizabeth, South Africa, stands as a tribute to the millions of horses that have suffered and died in man's quest for land and power.

One of the first references to horses crossing the Orange/Gariep River and entering present-day Namibia, and possibly also the first record of Europeans venturing into southern Namibia, appears in the records of Jacobus Coetsé Jansz's hunting expedition of 1760. He writes how he was able to use his horse to chase down and kill a giraffe, which he described as being 'a type of camel, albeit not the proper one'.

The indigenous people had no term for 'horses' in their vocabulary. The Herero would later refer to their horses by their colour or use the word for the hartebeest antelope *'oka-kambe'* or the zebra *'ongoro'*. As the South African colonial frontier expanded, it pushed people of Nama origin (the Khoikhoi) further north and eventually over the Orange River into Greater Namaqualand (southern Namibia). The Oorlam group, originally Khoikhoi in origin, had over time and with European influence changed their lifestyle and semi-nomadic existence, becoming traders, raiders and hunters, dependent on firearms, horses and gunpowder. (The term 'Oorlam' meaning 'experienced people' was possibly derived from the Malay term 'Orang lama'.) They settled in Greater Namaqualand amongst the Nama in the 1790s bringing their horses into the country with them. In the late nineteenth century, another group, the Basters (people of mixed descent originating from the Cape settlers and indigenous Khoisan women) migrated north in search of land. They were followed by the Dorsland (Thirstland) trekkers, Dutch settlers who left South Africa not wanting to live under the British crown. European hunters and traders also entered the country to see what opportunities lay sparkling beyond the borders.

From the 1880s and with the arrival of the German settlers to the arid African land, there was a steady influx of horses from the Cape and Europe. Imperial German stud farms were established at the turn of the century, the main one Nauchas, breeding with horses from England, Argentina, Germany and the Cape. The Cape horses were crossed with Thoroughbreds, Arabs and Hackneys bred for work and riding purposes, and for the German military troops, the Schutztruppe. In the 1904-1907 German-Nama/Herero wars, horses were imported from South Africa, Europe, Germany, Australia, Hungary and Argentina. A further influx of horses occurred at the onset of

The conflict between groups resulted in a huge influx of different horse breeds into south-western Africa.

the diamond rush in the south-western corner of the country in 1908. The lure of riches drew many a hopeful prospector and the area saw a huge demand for workhorses in the diamond fields and racehorses for the town of Lüderitzbucht. More and more stud farms began to appear in German South West Africa over the years including Kubub, Duwisib, Claratal and Voigtland, and the van Wyk stud farm in the Rehoboth area. The last large influx of Cape horses, brought in by the South African Union troops, was during the South West Africa Campaign at the time of World War I.

These two centuries of horse importation transformed southern Africa. Horses had a massive impact and influence before the advent of the motor vehicle. Horses, guns and gunpowder dramatically changed southern Namibia, socially and environmentally. The lifestyle of the local people changed from semi-nomadic pastoralism to trading, hunting and raiding from horseback, and from self-sufficiency to a dependency on Western commodities. There was an

enormous impact on the wildlife in the area, species like rhino, elephant, giraffe and a number of antelope species becoming extinct in southern Namibia over time. The power of the horse and the role it played in accelerating civilisation worldwide is often overlooked, yet the advancement of the modern age up until the twentieth century, in southern Africa as in Europe, was dependent on the use, abuse and exploitation of horses. Progress was ultimately carried on the horse's back.

In the desolate sands of the Namib Desert, however, the fate of a group of horses veered off in a different direction.

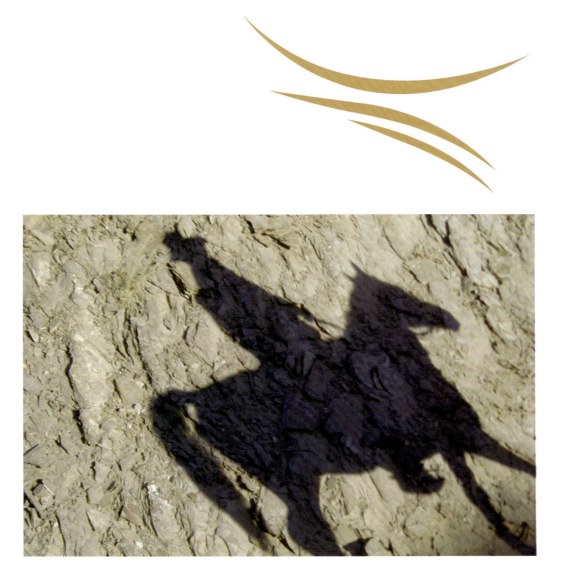

Lüderitzbucht in the early days

CHAPTER 2

THE PAST:
the arrival of horses in the namib desert

In south-western Namibia, the icy Atlantic Ocean fed by the Benguela Current lies in an intimate embrace with the golden sands of the ancient Namib Desert that languidly stretches up the country's coastline.

Scattered archaeological remains reveal that the Khoisan people had visited this bleak area through the centuries. The renowned Portuguese explorer, Bartolomeu Dias, docked at the 'little bay' now known as Lüderitz in 1487, calling it Angra Pequeña. Although the Dutch East India Company attempted to initiate trade with Nama groups in the area in the late 1700s and in the mid-1800s whalers, fishermen and guano collectors visited the natural harbour to reap her marine riches, it remained a desolate, barren coastline without fresh water. In the late nineteenth century however, the inhospitable corner of the country began the transformation that would culminate a decade later in a hive of colonial activity with settlements, soldiers and the excitement of a diamond rush. The colonisation of the south began in 1883 when the German trader Adolf Lüderitz visited the bay with his employee, Heinrich Vogelsang. In the following months Vogelsang, acting on behalf of Adolf Lüderitz, purchased the bay, a coastal belt running from the Orange River and an area into the interior from Nama captain, Joseph Frederiks. According to some sources, the price paid was £500 in gold and sixty Westley-Richards rifles. The deal was conducted in German geographical miles, *geografische Meile*, which are more than five times longer than English miles, a fact that Frederiks was apparently unaware of, subsequently disputing the agreement.

Adolf Lüderitz

Lüderitz returned to the Cape Colony to find the rights to his newly acquired land challenged. After lengthy negotiations and the arrival of a German gunboat to mark its presence in the bay, the British conceded that Germany could found its first colony there, a move that ultimately led to the existence of German South West Africa. With the German flag hoisted, the settlement began to grow. Adolf Lüderitz is said to have made little from the deal and eventually disappeared while out prospecting in 1886. It is thought that he drowned in the Atlantic Ocean somewhere between the Orange River mouth and Angra Pequeña, leaving the arena of history and the land tagged with his name to the colonial scramble for Africa.

Lüderitzbucht (Lüderitz Bay), as it was referred to in the late 1890s, developed slowly as a trading post. A transport route across the desert from Lüderitzbucht to Aus, 125 kilometres to the east, was established. Although a small sea water condenser was installed in the town, it was inadequate for the town's requirements and fresh water still had to be shipped in from the Cape. Without a railway and before the advent of the motor vehicle, horses and ox-wagons were indispensable for transport and the development of the town. Lüderitzbucht became an

The Bay Road between Lüderitzbucht and Aus

important supply post for the Schutztruppe in the 1904-1907 war against the Nama people and traffic along the route increased. The troops used this 'Bay Road' (*Baai Weg*), which was little more than an ox-wagon track, to advance from Lüderitzbucht to Kubub, Aus and Keetmanshoop. It was renowned as the most difficult stretch through the desert. Ten thousand horses, mules, oxen and camels, and 2 000 to 3 000 men are said to have used this road during the war. With only a few water installations along the route, the shortage of water and grazing made this an arduous journey, and the Bay Road was littered with animal skeletons.

Zacharias Lewala with August Stauch's favourite horse *August Stauch*

Because of the harshness of the terrain and the necessity of transporting supplies to the troops, a railway line was deemed imperative and constructed between Lüderitzbucht and Aus in 1906, reaching Garub station, 25 kilometres west of Aus, in September of the same year. There was still a shortage of water. People, the railway and locomotives were dependent on the condenser at Lüderitzbucht and the wells at Aus. Water in the Namib Desert was a scarce and expensive commodity. It was therefore essential to secure other water sources. The first boreholes were sunk at Garub in 1907, providing water for the steam trains and supplying water to Aus and Lüderitzbucht. Garub was one of the first water sources in the desert and a boon for the arid area.

The diamond rush began in a flash and frenzy of excitement when on 14 April 1908 a railway worker, Zacharias Lewala, found the first sparkling stone at Grasplatz, near Lüderitz, which was passed on to his superior August Stauch. The area glittered with adventure and promise and the town boomed with people arriving to try their luck and hoping to change their fortunes.

Small mining towns sprang up in the desolate sands of the desert. It was told that in Idatal (named after Stauch's wife), also known as Märchental and referred to as Fairytale Valley, diamonds were picked up by the handful as they glittered in the light of the moon. Photographs of the time reveal men crawling across the sand on their bellies searching for the prized stones. There was an enormous demand for workhorses, mules and donkeys for the bustling diamond industry and recreational horses for the new and wealthy elite of Lüderitzbucht. The diamond towns shipped in their material from Europe and the Cape Colony, and built fine houses, theatres, skittle alleys and hospitals. It is said that at Kolmannskuppe, on the outskirts of Lüderitzbucht, champagne was cheaper than water. Colourful stories are recounted of the time, one especially entertaining about a fierce German shepherd dog called Moritz belonging to Madame Zimmer of the Lüderitzbucht brothel. Moritz's duties included frightening away customers who were not willing to pay and guarding the diamonds that were hidden in the false floor of his kennel.

By September 1908, the German colonial government proclaimed a prohibited diamond area or 'Sperrgebiet', a hundred-kilometre-wide area between the Orange River and the 26 degree latitude, restricting prospecting and unauthorized entry into its borders. Five million carats were found in the proceeding years until production was interrupted by World War I.

The summer of 1915 in Garub

> '. . . If your ministers at the same time desire and feel themselves able to seize such part of German South West Africa as will give them command of Swakopmund, Lüderitzbucht and the wireless stations there or in the interior, we should feel that this was a great and urgent Imperial service.'

From British Government cable to Prime Minister Louis Botha of the Union of South Africa, August 6 1914

Champagne corks popped, spectators dressed in their European finery (women's hats adorned with ostrich feathers) clapped as imported race horses surged to the winning post. Lüderitzbucht was bathed in diamond glory. Elaborate German houses lined the streets, bars flourished and the Kapps Hotel saw more visitors than the local church. People bought champagne by the crate rather than by the bottle and men are said to have toasted by sipping the sparkling wine out of ladies' shoes. Horse racing was the social event of the new elite and important racing events often coincided with the arrival of a ship in the bay. When Emil Kreplin celebrated his 43rd birthday on 5 July 1914, he was at the highpoint in his career, a respected mayor of the town, often a master of ceremonies, owning and breeding the best race and work horses, and was rich with diamond wealth. Little did he know that the clouds of war were massing on the horizon, that war would break out a month later in Europe and during the following month Union troops would descend on the desert diamond town irrevocably altering destinies in their wake.

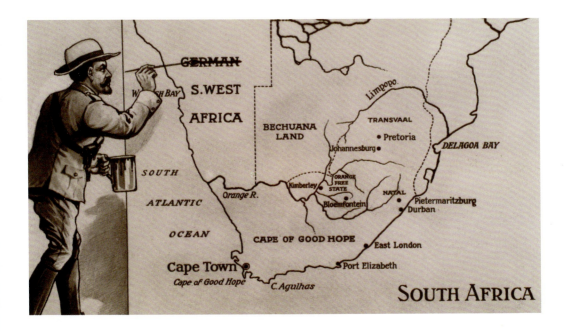

The Imperial invitation extended to the Union of South Africa to seize German South West Africa was 'cordially agreed' upon by General Botha and his colleagues. On 19 September 1914, when the Union forces landed at Lüderitzbucht, the German troops had already retreated inland blowing up the railway line behind them. When the Union forces' Captain De Meillon, head of reconnaissance, arrived with his advance party and approached a deserted house, they found hot coffee still standing on the dining-room table and the bed was still warm, luxuries he was not going to decline. The troops landed the following day in the town they described as an 'unpleasing place, bare of everything in the way of natural growth'. They hastily replaced the white flag raised above the town hall with the Union Jack. It was soon decided to send the remaining civilian occupants of Lüderitzbucht (not surprisingly referred to as 'obstreperous' and

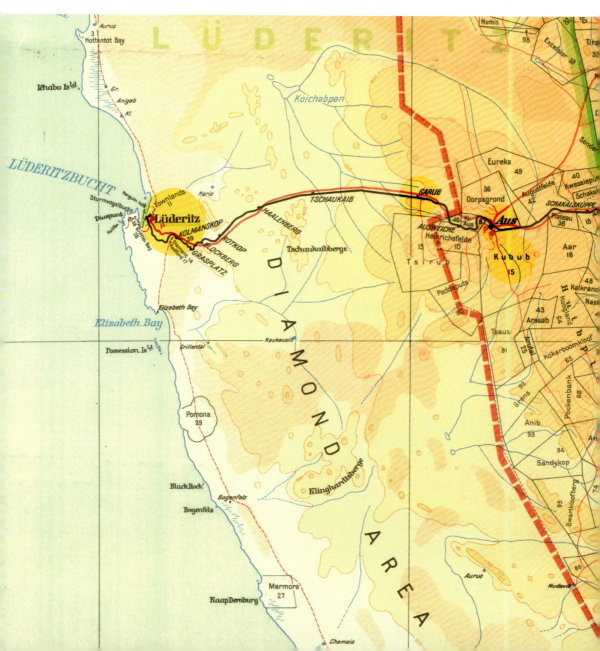

'cool' by the invading troops) to the Union for internment, *Bürgermeister* (mayor) Kreplin included. Although the original plan was for the Union forces to close in on German South West Africa from three different directions, the advance was suspended as a result of the rebellion in South Africa protesting the invasion. No other forces entered the country until the end of the year when the rebellion had been quelled. While troops stationed outside the town camped in the desert and worked under harsh conditions, battling the elements and repairing railway tracks and bridges, the Lüderitzbucht garrison made itself at home enjoying the comforts established by the German founders of the town. During the campaign some of the streets would be renamed, and the main thoroughfare Bismarck Strasse would become fondly known as King George Street.

After several months in the town, the days of gramophones and German music abruptly ended. The campaign was resumed and Union forces followed the German soldiers into the interior, inching forward, continually repairing the railway line, a lifeline in the desert ensuring the continuation of supplies from Lüderitzbucht. The rate of advance was limited by the shortage of water. Every drop of water required during the advance to Garub, 101 kilometres east, had to be condensed from sea water at the coast or transported by ship from the Cape. The largest transport vessel in the campaign, the SS Monarch, carried 4 000 horses, tons of fodder, supplies

Mounted Union troops crossing the Namib

and 750 000 gallons of Table Mountain water. Progress was extremely slow as the men battled the wind and heat, crossed deep sand and jagged rocks. One account succinctly describes the desolate terrain: *'The long treks across this God-forsaken country are like a hideous nightmare ... The country now is simply rock and sand, rock and sand... A few horses give in occasionally'*. The water from a few isolated wells, the desalination plant and the transport ships was not sufficient for all the men, horses and mules. The Namib Desert was aptly known as 'the thirstland' and with little action seen by the troops with the exception of the odd skirmish, the real enemy was the desert. The Germans had realised the strategic value of water and the railway in the desert conditions,

Union horses stationed at Garub

which they considered 'their strongest defence'. As they were hopelessly outnumbered, approximately 6 000 soldiers against 50 000 Union soldiers, they could only put up resistance where possible, lay mines and destroy railway infrastructure and boreholes to buy time and delay the inevitable. They poisoned wells and waterholes, either by throwing in a dead animal, animal entrails, carbolic acid, creosote or sheep dip. When Union troops reached an abandoned settlement, they had to first test the water from the wells for poison and had to repair boreholes before they could gain access to the life-giving fluid.

When the Union forces reached Garub on 22 February 1915, more than two months later, they found that the water tanks had been demolished, the station house had been torched and the railway to the east had been dynamited. The soldiers shouted through parched lips as they arrived, "Water, water." A trooper aptly reported about life in the desert: *'We breathed sand, we chewed it, we took it in our food, literally – there was sand in the sugar; we thought sand, we dreamed it'.* The boreholes were repaired and re-drilled, and the underground supply of potable water ensured that the 10 000 men and 6 000 animals were well-watered. The area around the boreholes was pounded into a fine powder that rose in an enormous dust-cloud as the animals in their thousands gathered to drink.

It was decided to build a narrow gauge railway loop to the boreholes from the station house to be able to fill the water trains. The four-and-a-half kilometre deviation turned out to be one of the most expensive strips of railway ever built, costing £75 000/mile, taking into account the time utilised and the cost of Union soldiers. It took nearly a month to complete, delaying the advance, and while it was under construction thousands of men with their animals stood idly by.

The German troops were stationed in the hills at Aus, 25 kilometres to the east. With an airfield, wireless masts, an intricate system of trenches and fortifications that ran through the hills, lookout posts and gun emplacements, they were well placed for defence and prepared to make a strong stand. Their plane flew before sunrise when it was easier to take off in the relative coolness of the morning. The German airman was affectionately referred to as 'Fritz', and after sighting him in the morning, the Union troops knew they were safe for the remainder of the day.

Fritz paid several visits to the Union base at Garub but only bombed it three times, the last being on 27 March, the summer of 1915, to mask the Germans' retreat, scattering about 1 700 grazing cavalry horses and causing untold havoc. When the Union forces from Garub reached Aus three days later, the German troops had already evacuated to the north to avoid being cornered by advancing Union forces fast closing in on them from the east and the south. Under the circumstances, they 'had no option but to abandon their fine fortifications'. The Union forces were therefore fortunate to avoid a hard fight, and the small town of Aus narrowly escaped becoming one of the main battlefields in the campaign. The strategic importance of Aus and the expectation of fierce resistance was epitomised by a soldier's report: 'Aus had always been a name to conjure with right from the time we had set foot in Lüderitzbucht'. After securing the water sources, they followed the Germans, hot on their heels.

The two forces eventually engaged at Gibeon bringing the southern part of the campaign to a close. The Germans surrendered on 9 July 1915 at Khorab, north-east of Otavi in northern Namibia, after several rounds of peace talks. German South West Africa fell under the Union of

German troops at Klein Aus

South Africa military administration until it was mandated to the Union by the League of Nations after the war. The southern African 'side-show' to the European war, which was still to continue for several more years, was over. In the proceeding weeks of evacuation, the area saw much traffic as troops, equipment and animals were transported back to Lüderitzbucht and the Union. Interned civilians from the Union and reservists from Khorab were allowed to return to their homes. A Prisoner-of-War camp was constructed on the plains east of Aus, housing 1 552 Schutztruppe soldiers. It was at this time of epic pandemonium that the horses which had been abandoned during the war period, and in the ensuing chaos, began to congregate at Garub.

Kreplin returned from his internment in the Cape in 1915 and resumed his life and duties in Lüderitzbucht, deciding to return to Germany in 1920 for health and personal reasons, following many of his countrymen who had left or been deported at the end of the war. His farewell party took place in the Kapps Hotel hall with many diamond magnates, including the renowned August Stauch, present. In gratitude for the years of service he generously gave the town, he was awarded honorary citizenship. He departed by rail to Cape Town and was set to sail via Holland to Germany. The entire town assembled to shake hands with him and wish him well as he boarded the train, with many a 'Hurrah, hurrah' trailing after him in farewell as the train steamed off into the desert.

Watering mules and horses during the campaign

Farriers at work in Aus

Garub then and now

Kreplin and his family surrounded by well-wishers at his farewell

Kreplin walking amongst his stud animals at the farm Kubub, near Aus

Emil Kreplin and the seesaw of life

Not many are familiar with the story of Emil Kreplin who was mayor of Lüderitzbucht from 1909 to 1920. His story is one of many, of people beginning with little, becoming extremely wealthy and ending up losing it all in the seesaw of life where it is possible to swing from being poor to rich and back again in the single flash of a lifetime. He was an autocrat, influential and instrumental in much of the social life and advancement of the town. He was also a central figure in the first hours of the diamond rush and the spark that set alight the area with diamond fever. As August Stauch's superior, he organised the locomotive and accompanied him to Aus to a Dr Peyer, superintendent of the railway hospital who maintained a well-equipped laboratory, for confirmation that the stone found by Lewala was indeed a diamond. He used a portion of his diamond riches to establish a stud farm at Kubub, near Garub, breeding workhorses and racehorses for the fledgling German colony and the surrounding diamond mines.

Kreplin was born in Barth, Pomerania, in Germany, apprenticed to be a blacksmith and joined the military as a professional soldier. He travelled with the Schutztruppe to German South West Africa in 1894 and was involved in the first fighting in the German colony against the Nama people. After twelve years in the service he returned to Germany. The country had entered his heart however, and he soon returned to work for a railway construction company, Lenz & Co, as an *Oberbahnmeister* (a railway supervisor). He was therefore at the right place at the right time when the momentous discovery of diamonds enabled men like him and Stauch to become remarkably wealthy almost overnight. He was one of the founders of Charlottental Diamantengesellschaft in 1908 and later on became the director of Kolmanskop Diamond Mines Ltd.

Emil Kreplin was such a prominent figure in Lüderitzbucht that it is recorded 'he practically controlled the place'. He played a crucial part in the negotiations with the German troops before they evacuated the town at the beginning of the South West Africa Campaign, convincing them to leave Lüderitzbucht intact. He was interned in the Union of South Africa when the Union forces arrived, for the duration of the campaign, afterwards resuming his life in Lüderitzbucht. He returned to Germany in 1920 for a ten year period, hoping to return to South West Africa at a future time, and visited some years later, in 1925. He told the local newspaper and townspeople who welcomed him on his return, *"It is good to breathe African air and spirit again, from the outer as well as the inner."* Kolmanskop Diamond Mines Ltd was placed in voluntary liquidation in 1923.

In Germany Kreplin lived in his house bought from diamond riches in the rural town of Wolzig on the outskirts of Berlin, appropriately referred to as Haus Lüderitzbucht (Lüderitz Bay House), known by locals simply as The Diamond House, but was unable to keep it through the depression years.

He returned to South West Africa where he bought a plot in Omaruru and started farming. In 1932 there was unusually heavy rainfall in the area and the Omaruru River came down in flood, taking his livelihood and last remaining pennies with it in its rush to the sea. Kreplin had finally lost everything. He went to Swakopmund to ask help from friends, and feeling abandoned and hopeless wrote a 'farewell forever' letter to his daughter Fritzi and shot himself in the heart on the banks of the Swakop River.

Kreplin and his wife, Frieda, mounted on two of his well-bred horses

Fritzi, Kreplin's daughter, on the Arabian stallion, Eddie

Kreplin with one of the donkey stallions used for breeding mules

FROM THE KREPLIN STUD ALBUM

The stallion, Billy, with Trakehner characteristics

A stallion with strong Hackney characteristics

A Cape mare (Boerperd) with a half-blood stallion

A step into the imagination

It only takes a small step of the imagination to visualise the scenario and the state of chaos in the area during the war period of 1914/1915. With a world war on their doorstep, it was a traumatic time for German South West Africa when many locals and farmers were forced to flee the volatile situation, leaving behind homes, farms and livestock. The war situation demanded that every available horse be used for the German war effort. As the Union forces landed on the southwestern shore, the German troops retreated into the interior. It wasn't long before the remaining local inhabitants were sent to the Union of South Africa for internment leaving their homes, lives and loves in German South West Africa. Gruelling months of pursuit through the desert followed when the armies may have abandoned lame or sick horses and stragglers to fend for themselves. Eventually, the soldiers reached Garub and Aus with their multitude of horses, and it seemed that full-blown confrontation was close at hand. Never again would so many horses be massed in this small section of the country as in the summer of 1915: 6 000 Union horses assembled at Garub, 1 500 German horses at Aus, as well as the additional horses from the Kubub stud farm.

As the German aircraft departed from the dusty encampment of Garub after dropping its bombs, the sound of the plane droning away into the heavens would have merged with the mayhem; panicked horses whinnying in terror, rearing amidst dust clouds and confusion, ears back, eyes large with fright, racing away from the army barracks and profusion of tents into the surrounding countryside. In their haste to pursue the Germans, the Union forces would not have had sufficient time to recover all of their horses. These would have gathered in the mountains initially where natural water holes held water at the end of the summer rainfall period, eventually making their way back to the permanent source of water at the Garub borehole when the pools ran dry.

It seems highly likely that stray horses formerly belonging to Emil Kreplin from the Kubub stud farm, approximately 35 kilometres southeast of Garub, made their way to Garub in the early 1920s, following good grazing after patchy rainfall in the area, joining the horses that were already massed there depending on Garub's water. Kreplin had leased the 50 000 hectare farm in 1911 from a Dr Paul Konrad Niethammer, a rich German industrialist who had bought the land from the Deutsche Kolonialgesellschaft for his youngest son to farm. At the time of the sale, the Deutsche Kolonialgesellschaft was taken over by the newly established government of German South West Africa, resulting in a dispute that dragged on until 1937 when the farm was finally transferred into the family's name. By this time Herr Niethammer had died, a world war had swept past and the country had fallen into the hands of the Union of South Africa. The farm, essentially remaining lordless, was leased over the years until it was sold in 1950 when the family felt the ravages of World War II.

The Kubub farm was in an elevated area safe from horse sickness, and being a fair distance inland from the desolate desert terrain of Lüderitzbucht enjoyed improved weather and grazing, and a supply of underground water. It was therefore an ideal place for the creation of a stud farm to provide horses for the bustling south-western corner. Kreplin was one of the first to bring in higher quality horses for racing and breeding purposes. Already in 1910, there are records of him introducing two Arabian mares into the Lüderitzbucht racing arena. Newspaper clippings praise his winning mare, Gala girl, for her first win. This affluent way of life changed abruptly after the

Horses at Kubub

outbreak of hostilities. Kreplin was interned for the duration of the South West Africa Campaign and later lost all his remaining wealth in the depression years that cloyingly dragged on the coat tails of the war in Europe. It is assumed that he wouldn't have had sufficient resources to attend to his assets in South West Africa, resulting in the abandonment of the Kubub horses. Ownerless, and without fences to contain them, the horses left to themselves would have begun to scatter in groups, leaving the Kubub area that had been overgrazed during the war period, following green grazing and water sources towards Garub, becoming wilder over time.

Photographic evidence of the Kubub stud farm (scenes with approximately 150 horses taken in 1912 and 1919), unearthed by hobby-historian Walter Rusch, reveal that there are remarkable similarities in conformation and characteristic markings between the Kubub horses and the present-day wild horses. The Kubub breeding stock would have comprised a large proportion of mares and foals, in contrast to the military horses which were probably predominantly geldings. As mares have a larger (sixty percent) influence on the gene pool, a significant amount of mares would have had to be part of the group assembled at Garub. From the size of the present-day wild horse population, it can also be deduced that a significant population of at least fifty horses or more, would have been needed to initiate the wild horse population in order to reach their present numbers. It therefore seems plausible that the Kubub horses constituted the core group of the wild horse population.

Some of the Kubub breeds evident in the wild horse population are Hackney, Trakehner and Shagya Arab. Interestingly none of the grey (i.e. white) genes have survived in the population, only the bay, chestnut and black remaining.

Later on, in 1984, FJ van der Merwe of the Department of Agriculture, South Africa, would write: 'The Namib Desert Horses are clearly not just any old farm horses turned loose, but something very special derived from the excellent gene pool that was existent in pre-1914 German South West Africa … '

The core group of stud horses, together with the Union horses from Garub, and horses abandoned by the Schutztruppe, Union troops, settlers, railway workers and others, would have formed the ancestors of the wild horses seen today at Garub and referred to as the wild horses of the Namib.

'In general appearance, the horses are of the hot-blooded type, i.e. they are athletic, well muscled, straight and clean limbed with exceptional bone quality, short backed, well shouldered, showing well-bred quality in the head, skin and coat. The bay to brown coat colours are very strongly represented with the occasional chestnut and apparently no greys.'

FJ van der Merwe, Notes on a Herd of Wild Horses in the Namib Desert, 1984

A comparison between the Kubub horses and the wild horses as they are today, highlighting definitive characteristics which indicate their ancestry

Origin theories

Wild horses of unknown origin encourage speculation and there are many alternate theories as to how they ended up in south-western Namibia. We cannot discount myth and mystery, or the need to entertain the mysterious in our lives. The origin myth involving a shipwreck appeared in the first articles printed about the horses in the late 1980s. The theory surmises that the horses were part of a cargo of domestic animals on a freighter that ran aground in the late nineteenth century, south of the Orange/Gariep River mouth bordering Namibia and South Africa. Any survivors, however, would have had to make an impossible journey across the Orange River and 200 kilometres of barren desert to arrive in Garub.

Another theory surmises that the wild horses originated from Duwisib Castle, 250 kilometres north of Garub, belonging to Baron von Wolf, and were released or escaped from Duwisib after the Baron's death in Europe in World War I. The more romantic version relates that his distraught wife threw open the gates to the farm in a fit of grief allowing the horses to run free. The likelihood of this theory is doubtful because it is in the nature of horses to stay in the area they are accustomed to as long as there is food and water rather than to migrate. Additionally, archival evidence reveals correspondence about the sale of Duwisib horses and horses trekking to Mafeking for sale in 1923. The records also show that there were over 200 horses at Duwisib in the early 1920s, and horses were still listed in the Duwisib books as late as 1940. The Garub horses had already made their appearance twenty years previously.

Crackerjack, one of Duwisib's famous stallions

**Horses played an important part
in the social life of Lüderitzbucht residents**

In the Safety of the Sperrgebiet: 1920–1977

When Kreplin boarded the ship to return to Germany, he would never in his wildest imaginings have guessed that his prized stud horses, bred for the diamond fields and the racetracks of Lüderitz, would initiate a wild horse population in the Namib Desert. The circumstances of the war culminating in the signing of the surrender on 9 July 1915 became the pivotal event that influenced many people's lives, transformed the country from German South West Africa to South West Africa under protection of the Union of South Africa, and ultimately led to the horses gaining their freedom.

The horses escaping the state of chaos in the area after the war lived in the protected Sperrgebiet diamond area which provided safety from hunters and horse capturers. The early establishing years of the horse group were good rainfall years and the permanent water-source at Garub (maintained for the railway) ensured their survival.

When the Union forces left Garub in pursuit of the Germans, attendants would have remained at the Garub borehole to maintain it and to pump water for the trains and for the town of Lüderitz which was dependent on Garub for fresh water. Once the war was over, the soldiers were replaced by South African Railway (SAR) workers. They would have watered their animals, simultaneously providing water for the horses.

In 1920 Sir Ernest Oppenheimer of the Anglo-American Company acquired the remaining diamond mines around Lüderitz and amalgamated them as Consolidated Diamond Mines (CDM), including those in the Sperrgebiet. The entire area remained a restricted diamond area until 1986, when a section of the Sperrgebiet was incorporated into the Namib Naukluft Park, allowing the population of horses around Garub to remain there with minimal human interference. Access was limited by the security regulations of CDM; the only areas where public movement was allowed being the railway line and the road.

After the war, when people returned to farming, the renewed agricultural activities would have pressurised the horses to remain in the safety of the protected diamond area.

The wild horses at Garub were first noted in the late 1920s. Passengers travelling between Aus and Lüderitz occasionally glimpsed the horses when the steam train stopped at Garub to replenish its water supply. A reliable source remembers the horses from her youth. She remembers that the locals, at that stage comprising many Afrikaans-speaking farmers who had made their way over the border from South Africa, referred to them as 'those German horses' and later as 'Garub horses'.

Another source describes the years of the 1920s, 30s and 40s when many people in the area still depended on horses, by saying, "*Hierdie wêreld was perde wêreld (This area was horse world)*." After

World War I, the mode of transport began to change and already by the mid-30s countless horses had become redundant, not being worked or handled regularly. People began to refer to horses left on farms as 'wild horses'. In the later years, one of the Kubub farm tenants reported killing wild horses on his farm for cooked pig fodder.

The Sperrgebiet was 'opened' periodically from the 1950s until 1983 at times of severe drought to drought-stricken farmers for emergency grazing. (In the south of the Sperrgebiet, emergency grazing was allowed before the 1950s.) There are reports during this time of horses with pieces of rope around their necks, presumably from people trying to catch them. A few horses are known to have been caught by farmers but they soon found that they didn't make suitable riding horses being of a small size (13½ to 14 hands) and wild in nature. Several carcasses were found in the desert, shot at random for no apparent reason. Horses were also shot when they entered the townlands competing with livestock for the scarce grazing.

The Namib wild horse population grew from the core herd. Several strays joined the group from time to time. A Mr Bolz from the nearby Klein Aus farm recalled how his horses of Duwisib stock used to stray to Garub and had to be routinely fetched and brought home. The single contributions would not, however, have significantly influenced the gene pool. The wild horse numbers have fluctuated between 50 and 280 horses in their 95 years of existence, droughts and the tough conditions of a desert life keeping their numbers low.

The South African Railways (SAR) maintained the railway line and the borehole and continued to pump water for the steam locomotives until the 1960s when diesel replaced steam. The pump-attendant then continued to pump water for the 'ganger' (a section foreman responsible for maintenance of the track) and his team who lived at the station, and for his family and animals, and coincidentally, the horses.

CHAPTER 3

a changing of perception:

1977 to the present time.

The horses had already been at home in the Namib Desert and the Sperrgebiet for almost sixty years when their existence was suddenly put in jeopardy. In 1977 Jan Coetzer, a security officer for Consolidated Diamond Mines (CDM), was patrolling the area when he noticed that there was no water in the Garub trough and horses were dying of thirst. Jan had witnessed this before on his patrols when the pump-attendant went on leave, did not work on public holidays or when the borehole had broken down. The ganger and his team at the station house, a few kilometres away from the pump station, had been removed as the railway sidings in the area were discontinued one after another. Diesel engines had replaced the steam locomotives that required a continuous supply of water and a tar road had been built linking Lüderitz with Aus. Workers were now transported to their destinations by truck rather than rail. The Garub pump-station broke down with increasing frequency as the equipment became older and maintenance workers had to be brought all the way from Keetmanshoop or Windhoek for repairs. The Garub water supply was no longer critical and water could now be delivered by truck.

When Jan passed through the area, he was concerned that without the need for water to be pumped daily, the pump-attendant would not continue to pump regularly and the horses would die of thirst. On his request CDM management appealed by letter to the South African Railways 'to ensure a continued supply of water' for the horses. An agreement was reached with CDM and SAR, with CDM paying a specific amount per month to ensure that the horses would remain watered. Jan installed ball valves (funded by CDM), allowing the trough to fill automatically, giving the horses 24-hour access to the water. Up until then it had been necessary for the pump-attendant to open a tap to fill the drinking trough. This had meant that even if water had been pumped into the reservoir, it wasn't accessible to the horses. Jan was transferred to Oranjemund in the early 80s but returned to replace the deteriorating reservoir with holding tanks and to install a new trough and ball valves.

In 1979, a large portion of the restricted diamond area Sperrgebiet II was ceded to the government for nature conservation and in 1986, the remainder of Sperrgebiet II and part of Sperrgebiet I, up to the Aus-Lüderitz road, was incorporated into the Namib Naukluft Park, monitored by the Directorate of Nature Conservation (which would become the Ministry of Environment and Tourism, MET, after Namibian independence in 1990). This included the largest portion of the horses' habitat, incorporating the water-point, and initiated a new phase in the existence of the wild horses as they now resided in a national park.

The Directorate of Nature Conservation took over responsibility for the horses and carried out the first aerial count, counting 168 horses, a number which increased in the good rain years of the late 1980s. A group of purists within the Directorate of Nature Conservation wanted to remove the horses from the Namib Naukluft Park in 1986, an idea that was strongly opposed by various people and wild horse supporters. These included people within the Nature Conservation body, the general public and Dr FJ van der Merwe, Director of Animal Production of the Department of Agriculture in South Africa, who had written the first report on the horses in 1984. Due to the strong outcry, no action was taken and the horses remained safely in the Namib Naukluft Park.

Dr van der Merwe obtained permission from the Directorate of Nature Conservation in 1987 to capture ten of the horses for research purposes. These horses were taken to the Veterinary Institute at Onderstepoort, in Pretoria, South Africa, for research on antibodies and water retention studies. They found that the horses had no antibodies against biliary or African horse sickness, and had no significant physiological adaptations to retain water, although they had acquired an increased tolerance to dehydration. Six additional horses were captured and transferred to Etosha National Park to be used by the Directorate of Nature Conservation as patrol horses, a plan that did not yield much success.

In the late 1980s, the entire eastern boundary of Sperrgebiet I and the Namib Naukluft Park from the Orange River to the Swakop River was fenced off with a game-proof fence. This measure reduced poaching and prevented game moving onto farmland, but also restricted the migration of game and made it impossible for the horses to search for grazing further east. Game had previously been lured onto farms and shot out in large numbers. Although the fence was a means to protect the wildlife, it restricted their movement and animals died along the fence in great numbers, an unintended consequence with a greater negative impact than the hoped-for protection.

What remains of Garub1 today

Wild horses at the original borehole in the 1980s

Oom Jan patrolling the Sperrgebiet

The original Garub borehole was used to provide water for the horses until the end of 1991 when new water troughs were built approximately four kilometres to the east, where they are presently situated at the Garub viewpoint. They utilise a borehole drilled by farmers for emergency grazing in the early 1960s, now belonging to MET. The borehole collects water in a reservoir from which

1991/2 drought

the troughs are gravity fed. The new water troughs have the advantage of being in an area with better grazing, visited more frequently by the horses and reducing the distance they have to travel from grazing to water.

It was also from this time that the horses began to feature in the media. In the late 1980s August Sycholt wrote the initial articles and produced a documentary on the horses. The first investigation into the population size and physical condition of the horses (as well as sheep) utilising the pasture was executed by a Senior Nature Conservation Officer, Chris Eyre, in 1985 and a report on the ecology of the horses was compiled by TC Meyer in 1988. In 1991, a French journalist, Jacqueline Ripart, camped at the original borehole for a two-month period observing the horses and in a report to MET noted that she had counted 276 horses. Although limited, her report was the first study on population structure.

In 1991/1992 a devastating drought spread through southern Africa and there were widespread attempts to rescue game throughout the region. When it reached southern Namibia, local people began to enquire about the starving horses and wished to sponsor food for them. MET decided to remove a number of horses to relieve pressure on the population. Because of inadequate information about the population, horses were captured randomly. One hundred and four horses were sold to interested horse owners at N$120 each. The horses were transported to farms around Namibia, seventeen being taken all the way to South Africa.

After the capture in June 1992, the remaining wild horses were given supplementary feed. The effort was sponsored by CDM, the Oranjemund Riding Club and horse groups in the UK, and included funds raised by Das Tier, a German wildlife magazine, and Charly's Desert Tours in Swakopmund. It was orchestrated by Jan Coetzer and the Oranjemund Riding Club and

The capture in June 1992

Some of the horses were darted for capture in 1997

implemented by MET. The horses were given food until it rained in March 1993 and green shoots of grass emerged. A hundred and fourteen wild horses survived the drought, while approximately sixty horses succumbed, mostly from the older and the younger age groups. They were survived by the strong middle core group. When the rains returned, there was soon ample grass and within a month the wild horses had regained their condition.

The captured horses however didn't fare as well, they had difficulties adapting to their new environments and domestic conditions. The horses that were translocated within Namibia into areas with similar grass species adapted relatively well, with the exception of those that were transported into areas of horse sickness and biliary. These were immediately susceptible to the diseases as they had no immunity-providing antibodies. The horses that went east struggled to adapt to their new environment, taking more than a year to gain condition. Even after receiving the necessary vaccinations, horses were still lost. Several horses, unaccustomed to being contained, were also badly injured in fences and camps. As far as could be traced, by 1997 at least half of the captured horses had died.

Public interest in the wild horses continued to grow. In November 1993, a look-out shelter was erected a hundred metres from the water troughs, allowing the public to view the horses. The road to the wild horses is located approximately twenty kilometres west of Aus on the B4. A one-

and-a-half kilometre gravel road leads to the viewpoint and hide overlooking the water troughs. From 1993 to 1994, Telané Greyling conducted a study on the behavioural ecology of the horses. After 1994, she continued visiting the area periodically for research and has kept detailed records of the horse population ever since.

The wild horse population increased slowly in the following four years of average to below average rainfall. In 1997 MET officials once again received permission to capture 35 horses from the population of 149. The horses were selected according to sex ratio and population composition in an attempt to minimise the impact on the population. They were removed to a holding facility at the Hardap Dam, 350 kilometres north-east of Garub, after which they were to be sold at a public auction. During the first six weeks however, problems began to develop in the behaviour of the horses with the stallions becoming increasingly aggressive in the confined spaces of the *bomas* (enclosures), something not seen in the wild population. Fortunately, the auction was cancelled and the horses were released back into the desert. As their hooves touched sand and home territory, they galloped off into the freedom of the desert.

In November 1997 it rained for the last time in a two year period. The drought of 1998 affected Namibia severely. By July 1998, the condition of the population started to deteriorate. Because rainfall cycles had been average to below average for the previous four years, there wasn't an adequate reserve of grazing for the horses. Once again the natural elimination of older and younger horses began to occur with the middle core group remaining. Eighty-nine horses survived the drought. If the proposed auction would have proceeded as planned, the horse population would have been reduced to a dangerously low level, exaggerating the severity of the bottleneck effect on the population and placing their future at risk.

While the 35 horses were in the boma at Hardap Dam, seven of the remaining horses died of dehydration when their water was accidentally shut off.

It was at this time that the wild horses' plight became known internationally. A film was being made outside Swakopmund portraying a story of the wild horses as narrated by a young colt, and referred to as 'Hoofbeats' but released with the title 'Running Free'. Articles published in the United Kingdom (Daily Mail and Evening Standard) and Germany about starving wild horses triggered an overwhelming response. The articles immediately prompted Columbia TriStar

Motion Picture Group to contribute a considerable amount to the Wild Horses Fund established by the Namibian Nature Foundation (NNF) to provide supplementary feed for the horses. Local businesses were amongst the many who generously donated. Public awareness and empathy for the horses grew worldwide and envelopes with banknotes flooded in from a wide spectrum of people from children to grandmothers.

The horses were provided with supplementary feed for a five to six month period. The lucerne was distributed by MET and spread widely to reduce the competition amongst the horses. In March 1999 the rains returned and fell on the parched thirsty earth.

The year 2000 heralded a decade of good rains. The horses spent more time at the water troughs becoming more habituated to people. Because of the good grazing in proximity to the troughs, there was no need for them to spend their time travelling to grazing areas and they had more time for social interaction, resting and playing.

The droughts and their devastating effect on the condition of the horses triggered worldwide public interest

Jan Coetzer - Custodian of the Namib Wild Horses

Jan Coetzer served as an unofficial custodian of the wild horses from the time he began to patrol the area for Consolidated Diamond Mines in 1966 until his departure from the area in 1981. He kept an eye on the wild horse population and regularly checked up on the borehole and the availability of water for the horses. When water was not pumped regularly, it was through Oom Jan's ('Oom', the Afrikaans word for 'Uncle' denoting respect) recommendation and effort that CDM communicated with SAR requesting a continued supply of water for the horses. When the pump broke down, he drove water out to Garub in a tanker. He ensured that the pump equipment remained in good working order, replacing the reservoir with holding tanks in the early 1980s and installing ball valves to fill the trough automatically. Oom Jan once again became involved in the wild horses' plight in the 1992 drought when he raised money for supplementary feed.

Jan Coetzer's father was born in South Africa and came to German South West Africa as a young man to fight in the war in 1914/1915, remaining in the country afterwards. Jan grew up on a farm adopting all sorts of animals and continued to care for abandoned animals, from springbok and gemsbok to owls and lanner falcon, throughout his life. He was appointed an Honorary Nature Conservation officer, nominated by Namdeb, for the Lüderitz/Oranjemund region. In this capacity he acted as a ranger and reported irregularities in the area.

He says that many people have contributed in different ways to the survival of the wild horses. He gives credit to CDM for supporting the continued existence of the horses in the protected and well-policed Sperrgebiet and to South African Railways for making the Garub water available for the horses.

A man who has always had a love for animals and especially horses, Oom Jan was attracted to the mystique of the wild horses existing in this remote area in extreme conditions and how they had become a pure breed through decades of isolation and natural selection, only the strongest of the population having survived. He describes how 'the challenge between two stallions can literally take your breath away as they paw the ground, prance, snort and rear, proud and free'. He says, "If you tame a wild horse, you take away some of its spirit."

Research and Reality: Clearing doubts and planning for the future

In 1999, after the 1998 drought, there were concerns raised by MET members about the predicted world-wide climate change that could alter the desert environment, rendering it even drier and therefore incapable of sustaining the horses. There was talk of relocating them to a farm where they would have access to better grazing as the horses' area in the Namib Naukluft Park is restricted by a fence in the east and south and the waterless desert in the west. There were also concerns that they were having a negative impact on the environment and displacing native species. It was decided that further research was needed to gain a proper understanding of the carrying capacity of the land, the biodiversity and the impact of the presence of the wild horses.

In the years 2003-2005 further in-depth research was undertaken by Telané Greyling as part of her doctoral thesis, looking at population dynamics, the influence of the horses on biodiversity, tourism activity in the area, plant communities, grazing capacity, termite grass utilisation and large herbivore densities and distribution. The research indicated that the horses do not displace any indigenous animals; they utilise an area at the edge of the Namib Naukluft Park that covers less than 0.7% of the total size of the Park. No evidence was found of significant interspecific competition between the Namib horses and the game in the area. Being less dependent on water, the game species have far greater ranges than the horses. The horses also do not have a significant impact on the vegetation. It was discovered that the lack of moisture rather than the impact of grazers controls the environment in the region.

A workshop was held to gain a clearer picture on the future management of the wild horse population and to formulate a management plan based on the findings. It was attended by representatives from MET, the veterinary services, the tourism industry and scientists from Namibia, South Africa and the United Kingdom. It was recommended that the horses should remain in the area, and not be relocated, with as little interference as possible, but that periodic intervention may be required. It was also recommended that the population should remain large enough to allow for the natural losses that occur during a drought period, these being old and weak horses and youngsters which may have some or other physical weakness. The carrying capacity of the land should be monitored to allow the population to fluctuate between a minimum and maximum threshold of between 50 and 200 horses. If a situation develops that could lead to the population exceeding the maximum or dipping below the minimum threshold, decreasing the herd to a point where it would affect genetic diversity, interventions should be employed to wisely manage the situation.

Embodying the spirit of Namibia

Namibia is referred to as a whole continent in one, mirroring all aspects of Africa. This mirror-ball of a country is a shining accumulation of attractions, including the Wild Horses, and intriguing destinations from the Fish River Canyon, the sensuous red sand dunes of Sossusvlei, to the wildlife of Etosha National Park.

It is a country of contrasts offering a magnificence of landscapes from the dry beauty of the Namib Desert to the lush waterways of the Caprivi in the far north-east. The country is especially appealing to people with a love for wildlife, desert scenery and the wide open spaces which characterise the country. The sparkling qualities which make it such an appealing destination are described as soulful, liberating, rugged, natural and free. These are the selfsame qualities which characterise the wild horses. The Namib wild horses embody the spirit of Namibia.

Tourism essentially began to grow in Namibia after its independence in 1990 when the preceding political turbulence settled and visitors felt assured of the stability of the new country. Tourist figures have since doubled a number of times. The wild horses have contributed to this increase, used as a generic marketing tool for Namibia on brochures and in films, encompassing the atmosphere and the virtues of this vast land.

Horses were brought to south-western Namibia for transport, work and recreation, by traders and settlers, eventually falling out of use for transport and labour, replaced by mechanisation and the modern world. The wild horses have since found a new and different type of function in tourism which contributes significantly to the creation of employment and the reduction of poverty, thus increasing the economic benefits for all Namibians.

Observing the wild horses from the Garub viewpoint, twenty kilometres west of Aus, has become a popular highlight when visiting south-western Namibia and tourist guide books include the wild horses as a recommended attraction in the area, with Lüderitz and the abandoned diamond mining town of Kolmanskop. Guided excursions are also offered to the tourist concession area. Visitors incorporating a stop at the wild horses into their itineraries, en route to or from the Fish River Canyon and on their way to explore the sand masterpieces of the Namib Desert, have the opportunity to inhale, absorb and exult in the wild beauty and free spirit of Namibia.

Visitors to the viewpoint should refrain from feeding or touching the horses, or venturing out of the hide into their area. The horses are unaccustomed to human food which can have detrimental effects on their digestive systems, and physical contact negatively affects their behaviour and carries the risk of injury. Please respect that the attraction of the wild horses is that they have minimal interference from people.

The Fish River Canyon horses

There is another population of Namibian wild horses that is often overlooked. A small group of wild horses in the very south of the country roam the canyon area from Sulphur Springs to Ai-Ais and down to the Orange River. They are sometimes encountered by hikers in the Fish River Canyon, and unlike the Garub horses are not dependent on humans for water, but drink from the puddles and pools of the Fish River as it makes its way southwards. They are exquisite apparitions seen as you turn a bend in the canyon, when the heat dazzles, the blue sky forms a canopy above and the green reeds and birdsong offer cool respite from long hiking days.

Their origins can be traced back to a farm in the canyon area called Kochas, situated between the main viewpoint and Ai-Ais. The farmer, a Mr Stoffel Pieters, persevered in trying to farm in the arid area in the severe drought of the 1970s. He applied to the government for an emergency grazing license to enable him to move his sheep to an area with better grazing. He was allowed grazing rights in the Warmbad Bondelswarts area where he resided for a few months with his sheep. It was there that he came across many horses. Horses had lost their status in the 1940s and 50s with the advent of cars and most people were happy to get rid of them, often giving them to their workers as remuneration. The farmer asked the Namas if he could purchase some of the animals, agreeing to pay R8 per horse, and took approximately thirty horses back to his canyon farm. As it was impossible to fence off the area, the horses soon became wild. In 1992, before he died and the farm was sold by his wife, his son attempted to catch them, rounding them up with his motorbike. Chance intervened and when on the last stretch, he crashed the bike in the rough terrain, breaking a collarbone. The horses became free once again.

Forty years after they were initially brought to the canyon, roughly thirty horses are still believed to exist. They live a tough life, evident in their rugged appearance, feeding on reeds and hard grass, preyed upon by leopard and suffering in years of drought. Out of the public eye, they lack the protection enjoyed by the Garub horses.

CHAPTER 4

wild horse behaviour

'I am wild by nature.'

There are many questions about the Namib wild horses that are often asked by visitors, some answered by supplying general Equidae information and others by exploring the behaviour of the Namib population. As so few horses today have the good fortune of living a natural existence, there is very little generally known about the habits of Equus groups living free in the wild, reminding us of how far removed domesticated horses are from their natural ways. This section gives a brief overview of the behaviour of the Namib wild horses, allowing the reader some insight into the characteristic behaviour and dynamics of a wild population.

The Essentials

Wild (and domesticated) horses have a life expectancy of on average 20 to 25 years.

A foal or youngster is referred to as a filly (female) or a colt (male) from one to four years old. From five years old, they are referred to as adults, either mares or stallions.

The horses eat and sleep throughout the day and night, in bouts. (This depends on available grazing.) In average conditions, they will generally sleep for one to two hours, eat for three to four hours and then sleep for one to two again, and so on, incorporating a visit to the waterhole in between, as well as other social interaction.

Mutual grooming, as exhibited by these two-year old fillies, establishes social cohesion

An adult stallion with an unrelated colt engaged in mutual grooming

In the middle of the day with no risk of predators, the horses feel safe enough to sleep deeply

They can sleep standing up or lying down. There are three levels of sleep: standing with locked knees (facilitated by the 'stay apparatus') which is a light sleep, also called dozing, where they retain an awareness of their surroundings; lying upright with their heads resting on the ground which is a medium-level sleep; and lying flat on their sides for a deep sleep. They often dream at this level.

Their diet is made up predominantly of grass, mostly *Stipagrostis obtusa* and *Eragrostis nindensis*, and some shrubs and herbs. They will also consume their dry nutrient-rich manure, a behaviour called coprophagy. Contrary to popular belief, ingested plant material is concentrated during the digestive process. As horses don't digest cellulose as effectively as ruminants e.g. cows which have four stomachs, the nutrient-rich manure provides a high energy food. The coprophagy exhibited by this population in the harsh Namib environment is an energy-efficient way of deriving nutrition. In domestic situations horses will also eat dry manure if the opportunity arises, but manure is generally routinely removed to avoid parasitic infestations. In the Namib Desert, parasitic infestations are limited by the dry climate. Foals, on the other hand, eat fresh manure to acquire the essential intestinal micro-organisms for digestion.

Depending on the rainfall, the horses utilise an area between 20 000 to 40 000 hectares in the southern Namib Naukluft Park. Rainfall in this area ranges from 0 to 200 millimetres per year occurring in scattered showers throughout the year, but averages 30 to 40 millimetres on the lower plains around Garub and up to 60 to 70 millimetres on the eastern slopes, near the Park boundary fence.

Green grass emerges five to eight days after ten millimetres of rain

The desert landscape transforms after exceptional rainfall

Horses often approach the water troughs at a gallop. Moments like these give us a glimpse of the energy, spirit and sense of freedom of the wild horses, making a lasting impression and etching themselves into the hearts and memories of visitors.

The horses' drinking frequency is influenced firstly by the amount of available grazing, and secondly by the prevailing weather conditions - a combination of temperature, wind and moisture.

Drinking patterns range from twice a day to once in 72 hours (every third day) in cooler temperatures i.e. below 30 degrees Celsius. They can survive without water for a maximum of six to seven days before severe dehydration sets in, resulting in death.

The water troughs provide the only source of permanently available water in the desert

The gestation period is eleven months and foals generally nurse up to one year. Foals are born throughout the year in the Namib population because there is summer and winter rainfall, and the temperatures are also not as consistently cold as the European winters. The mares respond to the green grazing after rainfall by coming into season.

Population numbers fluctuate over the years. The Namib wild horse population has ranged between 50 and 280, with the present population tallying 200.

The first day in a foal's life

Social Structure

Social structure benefits animals in many ways, synchronising behaviour, providing protection from predators, an arena for the different sexes to meet and reproduce, and a relatively stable structure in which to raise their young.

Breeding groups standing in the vicinity of the water troughs

A group of bachelors gathers near the water troughs

A small breeding group: a stallion, mare and foal

The Namib wild horse population is comprised of breeding groups and bachelor stallions. A bachelor stallion is a stallion that has no mares at that particular time; a bachelor group is a group of bachelor stallions.

A breeding group comprises one or more stallions and one or more mares. It can also include one or more fillies that are not related to the group but have dispersed from other groups, as well as colts and fillies from the mares in the group, and 'outsider' stallions.

An outsider stallion contributes to the cohesion of the group, protecting the group by acting as a barrier. He may interact with the fillies and colts in the group but is prohibited from interacting with the mares. The outsiders move with the breeding group, but remain on the periphery.

A breeding group ranges in size from two members, a mare and a stallion, to as many as fifteen members. (In other wild horse populations, groups of twenty or more members have been recorded.)

Depending on the population size, the number of breeding groups at any one time can range between 20 and 35.

There are generally four kinds of breeding groups: A single stallion and mare/s and her/their offspring; a single stallion and mare/s with her/their offspring with one or more outsider stallions; two co-operating stallions and mare/s with her/their offspring; and a co-operating group with the addition of outsider stallions.

The fillies usually disperse i.e. leave their mother/parental group when they come into season for the first time, at approximately eleven months of age in good rainfall years, and seek out a

One of the larger breeding groups is visible on the left hand side with its outsider stallion on the right, and a small breeding group in the background

stallion. They travel back and forth between their group and their chosen stallion for several days to be covered and then either transfer to the new group or remain with their original group, only to disperse later.

The colts' dispersion varies depending on group dynamics and the particular circumstances of the time. Generally, they disperse between three and four years of age, but this can vary from between one to six years. They usually join other older bachelor stallions for the first year or two, showing signs of becoming part of a breeding group as an outsider or acquiring their own mares at five to eight years of age. (Exceptions have occurred, however, where a younger stallion has acquired mares.)

There is a continual natural flux in breeding groups, although they remain relatively stable in good years, with the usual changes including fillies dispersing, groups splitting and mares moving from one stallion to another. The group stability, and therefore the foal survival rate, is however drastically affected by a significant reduction in population size due to drought or capture.

Within this natural flux there are strong social bonds formed between individuals, often enduring for a lifetime, surviving through environmental and social challenges.

It's Not Black and White

Although it is generally accepted by most people that there is a dominance hierarchy (i.e. a pecking order) in wild horse groups, observation of the Namib wild horses has revealed that this terminology is too rigid to describe wild horse behaviour and it is often a matter of interpretation. Wild horse behaviour is far from being black and white, it varies considerably from day to day, from group to group and according to the circumstances of the time.

Dominance is often understood in terms of competition for resources. In the Namib Desert, the horses don't compete for resources with the exception of water at the drinking troughs, which is not a consistent competition. How determined a horse is to reach the water troughs seems to rather depend on how thirsty he is, regardless of 'social status', and the dynamics between groups and individuals around the troughs vary considerably.

In some instances a whole group may drink together if no other groups are present at the troughs. If one group is busy drinking, new arrivals will walk straight in to drink if there is enough space at the troughs or wait their turn, if not. The stallion of the present group may or may not interrupt his drinking bout to interact with the arriving stallion/s while his mares continue drinking. In some groups, certain individuals may be more wary than others and will not walk straight in to drink but rather circle or wait for a while. External circumstances such as wind and game present at the troughs will also influence the horses' behaviour.

Leadership is often thought to relate to dominance and aggression. However, this is a wide area and there are many interpretations and types of leadership. It is often accepted that a dominant animal (usually the most aggressive) is the leader of the group, but this is not necessarily the case. Examples from the various groups reveal extremely interesting behaviour patterns. Breeding groups with two co-operating stallions are a phenomenon where the stallions do not displace each other but rather co-operate within the group. Even competition for mares is minimised because each stallion has his own preferred mare/s. The types of relationship between co-operating stallions also vary, with some stallions having more intimate bonds because they grew up together or have been bachelors together for a prolonged period. In other cases, two breeding groups merged due to bonds between mares and the stallions of these groups therefore tolerate each other with minimal interaction. In some groups, one stallion may have a stronger presence than the other and may lead by initiating the movement of the group, but will not necessarily walk in front or protect the group; while in another group, an outsider stallion may walk in front of the group to the water troughs or away, yet does not initiate movement or lead the group in any way.

Interesting behaviour can also be seen amongst the mares. The phenomenon of a lead mare occurs in some groups, but not in all the groups, and only for certain periods of time. Mares with foals at foot will tend to follow rather than to lead. There are examples of bold mares that walk in front of the group to drink and initiate movement in the group, while there are also examples of more timid mares that may be more suspicious and careful when approaching the water troughs. The sequence changes and often varies. In certain groups, a mare will take a leading role while the main stallion of the group will remain behind the group as a protector. This may change over time. In some cases the stallion will be the leader as well as the protector of the group.

Body Language

Horses use a wide range of visual signals for communication. There are various types of body language, encounters and interaction amongst the horses. The more well-known ones being displayed by the stallions: posturing, the greeting ritual, the dung-pile ritual, fighting and herding.

Posturing: Posturing is exhibited to enhance the horse's outline for it to appear larger than life. The horses arch their necks, lift themselves to appear larger and more impressive, and move with cadence as if floating above the ground.

The greeting ritual: Most of the stallion encounters consist of a greeting ritual or a dung pile ritual and usually begin with posturing. They occur when two stallions, either from breeding groups or bachelors, pass each other, approach the water troughs at the same time or stand around the troughs. For the greeting ritual, two or more stallions will advance towards each other, stand with a nasonasal investigation, a combination of inhaling and exhaling, often with an accompanying snort. One or both may squeal or strike with a front leg. This is more of a demonstration than a fight, not intended to do bodily harm, and as the horses don't stand head on, they easily avoid the strikes. They may also push with their noses into the flank of the other horse or shake their heads. On occasion, after the initial greeting of inhaling and exhaling, the stallions will turn and walk away, or the interaction may end in a spin and a kick.

Dung pile ritual: If there is a dung pile nearby, the two stallions will approach it individually, sniff, step over it, add their own manure to the pile and then sniff it again. This is also done by a stallion while the other looks on or approaches. Sometimes they may sniff the pile together, often resulting in a squeal or a strike. The dung pile ritual often occurs in conjunction with posturing and the two together are a display of strength and presence. It is not always part of a display however, as the dung pile ritual will also be executed by a single stallion when he is on his own. As the horses are not territorial, the dung pile ritual is not a behaviour used to mark territory, but rather seems to serve as an 'information board' providing information about which horses are in the area, their diet, health etc.

Sometimes horses may sniff the dung pile together, often resulting in a squeal or a strike

Fighting: Fighting between stallions mostly occurs when one stallion invades the space of another stallion or the stallion's group at the water troughs, or when there is an available mare in the vicinity. It is usually more of a show without bodily contact and consists of a lot of quick rearing with very little contact. Often, the stallions will rear making no contact at all and then separate. If there is a serious fight, bodily contact will occur, with the horses rearing, chopping with the front legs and trying to bite each other on the neck, possibly positioning a leg over the other horse. They will sometimes bite and grab the other's neck with their one leg positioned over him and shake, which may result in serious injury.

After rearing, one stallion, seemingly the victor, usually chases after the other stallion for a short distance. He then continues to posture back and forth, positioned between the contested mare and the other stallion, occasionally chasing after his adversary again until the vanquished horse keeps its distance. Fights can last from less than a minute to several days in exceptional cases.

Colts will often engage in play fighting. This is also seen amongst stallions of all ages.

They can also involve more than two stallions. Occasionally, up to eight stallions will run in a pack after a single mare, biting and kicking amongst each other, rearing and falling out along the way.

Playing: often looks similar to fighting but the movements are slower with a lot more body contact and the horses' ears are not flattened against their heads, a clear sign to distinguish between the two.

Typical herding behaviour

Herding: When a stallion wants to move a mare or a group of horses in a particular direction, he will herd her/them by lowering his head, flattening his ears and moving his head in a gentle snaking motion. This can be such a subtle movement that the action of lowering his head on its own may attract the attention of the group or the horse he is trying to herd and initiate movement.

Herding can be seen in a variety of situations; a stallion may try to herd group members to the water or away when at the troughs and they are dawdling or departing before he's done, or to herd his group away from the possible threat of other stallions. He will also herd a lone mare or filly to incorporate her into his group. Herding may be seen in the case of an older bachelor stallion that takes a younger bachelor into his care.

General body language: A horse quite noticeably stiffens its body if it is not comfortable with another horse approaching, while it will soften its body if comfortable with a horse's approach. If its body-stiffening is not sufficient to deter another horse, it will then flatten its ears against its head, giving a quick look that very clearly conveys a 'Go away' message.

The horse on the left is flattening its ears conveying a clear 'Go away' message

A mare is indicating her disapproval of a stallion's approach

A friendly greeting between a stallion and a filly

The horse may also angle its hindquarters slightly to thwart the approach and it may cock its leg to indicate that a further approach may provoke a kick. Either a head threat or a kick threat may be used depending on the direction from which the other horse is approaching.

If a youngster (0 to 2/3 years) approaches another horse, it will lower its head slightly and stretch out its neck towards the other horse, pulling its lips back and exhibiting a chewing or jaw action sometimes referred to as 'mouthing'. It is an action used to appease another horse without initiating an aggressive response. It can be seen in instances when a foal is lost and trying to find its mother. The foal will first approach other horses while mouthing until it locates its mother. Mouthing can also be seen amongst yearlings and two year olds when they are approached or if they approach other horses e.g. when they are at the water troughs.

Courtship interaction between a mare and a stallion is non-aggressive and non-vocal in comparison to stabled domestic horses. In general, the mare will only kick at the stallion if she is not receptive or ready. Forced copulations occasionally occur during periods of drought and stress and usually involve young fillies that may incur fatal injuries.

Smell conveys messages in the animal world and plays a role in the social lives of horses.

Horses' keen sense of smell enables them to track other horses.

Horses exhibiting the flehmen response

Flehmen: When exhibiting the behaviour known as the flehmen response, a horse will curl the upper lip, drawing air over the vomeronasal organs which are located under the floor of the nasal cavity. It is mostly stallions that show this response to detect the odour of a mare in oestrus. Mares can also be seen exhibiting flehmen when analysing strange new smells, although it is uncommon for mares in the wild as they rarely come across new stimuli.

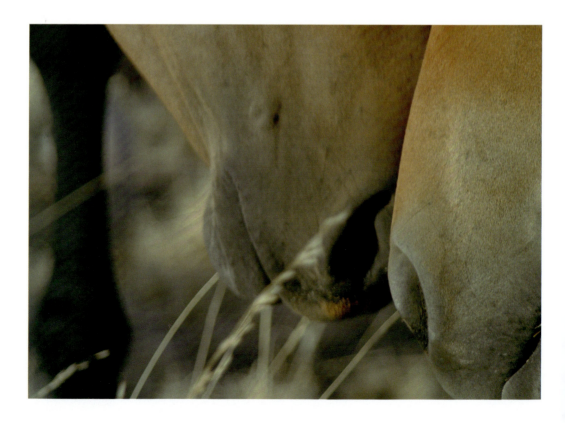

Risks, threats and survival

The essential act of being alive comes with a certain amount of risk. As with all wild animals, young and vulnerable individuals are seen as potential prey by the predators in the area. Other factors such as complications in birth and injury are potential fatal occurrences of daily life.

In the first two days of their lives, foals are more susceptible to fatal dangers. If stallions approach a mare with a foal, she may attempt to kick at them to protect her young, her movement or the stallions' reaction accidentally bumping the foal. This may cause internal injuries leading to death within the first two days. Injuries may also occur at times of instability in the group when a vulnerable young foal stands a greater chance of being bumped in the interaction between horses.

In the first two weeks of its life, the foal would also be susceptible to dehydration and exhaustion if the horses were walking long distances to find grazing. If the foal was unable to keep up, it would soon dehydrate because it would not be able to obtain sufficient nourishment from its mother.

For the first three weeks of a foal's life, the mother is very protective and attentive. After that she reaches a stage where she allows the foal to be more independent. The foal is then required to

follow the group. In the day-to-day events when the group departs an area, the horses will start walking away and the mare will stand a short distance away waiting for her foal to catch up. Occasionally, if there are many horses around, the foal can become confused or if the mare walks off too far, the foal may be unable to find her. If the foal is separated from the group, the chance still remains of it successfully locating its mother again. These incidents may occur in the foal's life between the age of three weeks and one month.

There have been incidents when a foal has been separated from its mother and adopted by a bachelor stallion that takes care of it. Because he cannot provide nourishment however, the foal's condition soon deteriorates and predators such as black-backed jackal and spotted hyaena are quick to target the foal as vulnerable prey.

Up until six months old, foals are potential prey to spotted hyaena due to their smaller body size. Hyaena are cautious of healthy larger horses.

Spotted hyaena await the death of their already mutilated prey, a month-old foal

Amongst the adult horses, several life-threatening possibilities exist:

- Occasionally, mares may have difficulty foaling, a condition called *dystocia*, when the foal is not positioned correctly in the uterus.

- As the B4 main road traverses the horses' habitat there is the risk of motor vehicle accidents, especially between dusk and dawn.

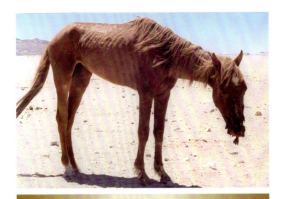

An unsuccessful hyaena attack

During the 1998 drought, the horses were supplemented with lucerne.

- Stallions are occasionally injured in fights and all horses risk injury through freak accidents. These injuries may include bone fractures, which are not in themselves fatal and often heal, but may lead to fatalities due to secondary causes. The horses can usually overcome and survive the lesser injuries. Animals that are weak from injuries will quickly be recognised as prey by predators.

- There may also be the rare occurrence of a horse eating a poisonous bulb or having an intestinal problem.

Although there is an adequate supply of grass, this mare is malnourished due to old age and because she has a foal at foot.

In times of drought when the quality of food is insufficient to sustain the body, the horses are weakened by malnutrition which together with social stress, poor organ function and botfly infestations can cause mortalities.

They will also suffer from malnutrition in old age even if there is an adequate supply of good food because they often cannot masticate their food properly and their bodies are unable to absorb and utilise nutrients effectively. Although intestinal parasites are not usually a problem, the possibility of botfly infestations are increased in old and weakened horses suffering from malnutrition and may contribute to the death of a horse.

The lean and the fat years

As the wild horses live in a desert environment, it is the rainfall and the resultant grazing which affect their lives. The revolution of the seasons and climatic patterns over the years have kept the wild horse numbers within certain threshold limits, allowing them to adequately survive on the land without exceeding the carrying capacity of the area. They live according to the rhythms of the natural world.

The 1990s brought times of drought to the land and the 2000s, a time of plenty. In the 90s, 1993 to 1999, the rainfall was average to below average, and it was above average from 2000 to 2010.

During the dry period, up to half the foals did not survive. The fillies were affected by either not coming into season or not conceiving, and only foaling for the first time when they were three to five years of age in contrast to two years of age when conditions are suitable and grazing readily available. They also dispersed i.e. left the parental group, at a later date. The horse population generally spent less time at the waterhole, coming in to drink and leaving soon after to spend more time grazing and travelling to grazing areas rather than spending that time in social interaction, mutual grooming and rest.

From 2000, the foal survival rate was ninety percent and fillies came into season at eleven months. They usually disperse when they come into season, either the first or second time. During the fat years, the horse groups spend a prolonged time at the troughs, drinking more often, sometimes more than twice a day, resting, sleeping and playing.

In these years of good grazing, there is a natural cohesion in the group fostered by the time spent interacting at the water troughs. Less friction is evident and the groups are more tolerant of each other. (The only abnormal behaviour seen in the horse population is when the horses are stressed in times of drought or when captured.)

When there is less grass, the horses drink less frequently because they are out grazing or travelling to find good grazing areas. They come to drink on average every thirty hours in hot temperatures and can have intervals of up to three days between drinking periods in cold temperatures.

Sex ratio, breeding success and the gene pool

'... the recurrent reduction in numbers during bad drought spells had the effect of distilling out the most hardy genes from the original, probably cross-bred population.'

FJ van der Merwe, The Real Namib Desert Horses, 2001

The gene pool of the Namibs is of considerable interest as they are considered by many to have forged a distinctive breed over the last century. Fears of inbreeding can also be laid to rest as research has shown that the horses generally avoid inbreeding because fillies disperse to an unrelated stallion, and the mares won't allow their colts to cover them.

There are equal amounts of male foals to female foals born in the wild horse population i.e. the birth-sex ratio is 1:1. The population-sex ratio is male biased however, i.e. there are more stallions than mares in the population. This is due to the mortality rate being higher in mares in stressful times such as in below-average rainfall periods because they have a higher energy output in raising foals and because of the risks of foaling. The male-biased sex ratio creates a situation where there are a greater number of smaller-sized breeding groups giving a larger number of stallions the opportunity to contribute to the gene pool. (If the population-ratio was female biased, the breeding groups would be larger but fewer.)

Not all horses have the opportunity to contribute to the gene pool as they are not all successful breeders. Some mares may produce more foals with a high survival rate, therefore contributing to the gene pool, while other mares may produce foals that either don't survive or don't continue breeding. The same can be said for some stallions that may sire more foals that become successful breeders while others tend to sire foals with a predilection to becoming bachelor stallions or mares that aren't successful breeders. Only approximately sixty percent of the mares and forty percent of the stallions contribute to the gene pool. It is therefore important to retain a large population.

Adaptations to the Namib Desert

The ability of the predecessors of the horse to adapt their behaviour to the changing environmental and planetary conditions over periods of millions of years, most probably contributed to their continued evolution and to the Family Equidae surviving up until the present day.

Equus caballus is one of the few species that is able to survive in a diverse set of conditions from desert to marshland on almost every continent in the world.

The Namibs exhibit this ability par excellence. They have not adapted physiologically to their challenging environment but have rather adapted their behaviour to enhance their survival in their desert extremes, their grazing and drinking patterns varying with the seasons.

The Namibs are accustomed to and tolerate dehydration, whereas domesticated horses would find a similar situation extremely stressful. This reduces the time needed and the energy expended in travelling to the water troughs, maximising the time available for feeding.

Signs of dehydration and rehydration are visible in the same horse before and after drinking

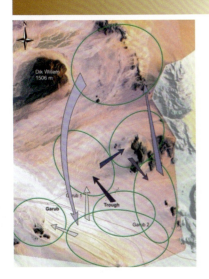

They adapt their behaviour when there is less grazing available by extending their grazing periods and reducing the time spent sleeping or playing, and vice versa in periods of abundant grazing.

They travel to areas with increased food resources according to the rainfall.

As also seen in other wild horse populations, their behaviour includes more posturing and displaying rather than aggressive contact, thus reducing the amount of serious injury.

The importance of social interaction and space for social interaction is often overlooked in the domestic horse world. Although the Namib Desert may appear a hostile environment, it fulfils the most essential needs of the horses, providing food, water and space.

the dream

'I have a dream.'

Martin Luther King

At the end of the day, the pale grass and desolate landscape glow with deep gold and copper hues as the sun begins its descent from the heavens, and then absorbs the more ethereal colours, the pinks, rose and purples of the sunset.

We have returned to the water troughs for the second time in the day, a blessing in this time of plenty. The colts play in the shadows that fall on the earth like soft gentle hands, and the relative coolness of the day and hushed atmosphere allow me the translucent and transient moment for reverie.

My thoughts tumble into the future and for a brief time I leave my present life as a black stallion standing proudly and resolutely in the magic of the sunset colours and I dare to dream.

As wild horses our lives are intimately intertwined with the cycle of the seasons. We are keenly aware that the fat years blend into the lean, of the balance that is maintained through both, and we choose to live with minimal interference accepting the natural order of life as wild horses of the Namib Desert.

I have a dream … Because our terrain is bordered by fence and desert restricting our ability to migrate and seek grazing elsewhere, at times of severe drought we recognise the need and benefit of accepting food supplementation. It has been proven through time that as wild horses of the Namib we don't fare well in domestication or capture. If our numbers increase to such a degree that it becomes necessary to remove horses, we don't want our fellows scattered and ending up abused in unsuitable homes. We wish to remain together. We have partners, foals and familial bonds. To keep our gene pool viable, I dream of a Namib Wild Horse custodianship programme where satellite populations will be developed and maintained to help ensure the conservation of the gene pool. The genetic material can thus be controlled and exchanged. Ideally, a piece of land in the nearby vicinity would host the initial satellite population.

As we near a hundred years of existence as a wild population, we are increasingly being referred to as 'the Namibs', the wild horses of the Namib Desert, a Namibian breed refined, strengthened and tempered by the test of survival in our desert environment. Like our human counterparts, our ancestors arrived from far-off places by chance and made this south-western corner of Africa and more particularly this arid land their home. It would be appropriate to commemorate a century of our adaptation to the desert environment and wild living as a tribute to the part we've played in the history of Namibia.

I dream on, imagining centenary celebrations where the Namibs are acknowledged as a national treasure, custodianship programmes and a Namib Horse Foundation, and see it all hovering before my eyes in the realm where all things shimmer with possibility and promise. It blurs momentarily, and I find myself back in my strong stallion body. It's time to lead my mares and colts away from the water troughs and into the deepening colours of the day.

A family group comes in at a trot whinnying, raising dust which scatters like gold flakes in the dying light. Another leaves and disappears into the descending darkness. At this time of the day and in this season of abundance, dreams and reality are one and our lives simply move with the stately pace. The wings of darkness embrace the day, the stars shimmer and shine and a buttermilk moon rises in the heavens to light our way forward to tomorrow.

APPENDIX

THE CHALLENGE:
Finding the balance between the norm and the natural

Bridging the gap between what we have learnt from the past and its application to the future will be a challenge that will inevitably be met as the cycles of the years once again turn and drought returns periodically to scorch the land.

Much has changed since the previous dry years that transformed the perception of the wild horses from feral to flavour of the month, putting them in the international spotlight and onto the Namibian map. More than that, however, with public pressure there has been a shift of thinking from toleration inside a national park to respect as a unique breed, a tourist drawcard and national treasure which has a century-old role in Namibian history. People are now ensuring the Namib Wild Horses' long-term survival.

But what have we learnt from the past and how will we face the future with the best interests of the wild horses in mind? It has been proven twice in the last twenty years that capture has placed extreme stress on the wild horse population and that the sale to private farms had disastrous consequences for the horses, as well as decreasing the population to its lower threshold where genetic diversity was at risk of reaching dangerously low proportions. Besides disrupting the existing population, the horses sold were on the most part unable to adapt to their new surroundings and were not suitable work horses. It was revealed in a relatively short time that owning a wild horse is a contradiction of terms. The horses prove remarkably adaptable and strong in the wild, their natural environment, but not in domestic situations.

We have however, also had these two decades to gather invaluable in-depth information on the population. Every horse can be individually identified and the dynamics of breeding groups are carefully recorded as they fluctuate with the freedom of wild *Equus* groups. Not only the population but the environment has been studied and it has been positively ascertained that the horses do not negatively impact the environment nor displace other animals. With this knowledge and the massive weight lifted from the destiny of the population, we can move forward to the next crossroads that awaits us.

It has been gauged from this past experience that besides certain management practices such as supplementary feeding in times of drought, the animals are best left to the ways and rhythm of the natural world with minimal interference. As in other populations of wild animals, this infers that older and weaker animals will die in lean years and reminds us that for wild animals death is a natural part of Life. Natural selection translates as Nature's own management plan, regulating numbers and eliminating the weak individuals in drought periods that are survived by the stronger horses, ensuring a strong gene pool. Drought is therefore not seen as a negative aspect but a natural occurrence. (Too much rainfall is often not beneficial, enlarging the population to exceed the carrying capacity of the land.) Will the public, private sector, general people of Namibia, visitors and the media remember this when the dry days arrive, and will they remember, recognise and understand that natural selection is what being wild and free entails? Even with supplementary feed, nature will still take its course and there will still be fatalities. It has been agreed that intervention will only occur if numbers appear likely to reach a critical point endangering the population. It is essential to recall that it is these very same experiences of natural selection, or 'survival of the fittest', which have tempered the horses over a century of survival, creating this tough, well-adapted Namib breed.

The horses have historical and cultural importance, being descendants of those that shaped the country, and have indirectly impacted all Namibians' lives. Acknowledging and accepting them as part of our culture and as a tourist attraction, however, involves a responsibility to protect them. The challenge is to strike a friendly balance with Nature, between what we consider the norm and the natural.

The 'norm' is an unspoken agreement, a standard set that is regarded by the majority as typical. For horses today it often means being kept in solitary stables in urban areas, far removed from their natural lives. 'Natural' means living in accordance with the natural world.

What practical long term solutions can we find to reach this balance with Nature? We can start with mineral supplementation if the grass quality is low to prevent the horses suffering from malnutrition. We can look forward to finding suitable land for satellite stations outside the main population to safeguard the gene pool. Other possibilities include contraceptive methods, already practiced in other wild horse populations, which will offer a low-stress solution to overpopulation. And, importantly, recognition and legislation of the Namibs as a national treasure and national horse will allow the horses' long-term protection. A starting point and a stepping stone across the large river is the formation of the Namib Horse Foundation which will in effect make the rest of the journey possible.

As the inception of the Foundation is a new concept that requires nurturing and support, we are running against time. From past records, this drought period should already have begun and we have somehow been allowed three additional years of plenty. If no rain falls by the end of the next summer, statistically the new drought period will be upon us and the Namibian land will be feeling the effects. Will we allow for the balance?

ACKNOWLEDGEMENTS

Heartfelt thanks to the following for their support:

The Swiegers family, Klein Aus
The Gondwana Collection
Jan Coetzer
Walter Rusch
CDM (Namdeb)
Mr and Mrs Greyling
Kobus du Toit
FJ van der Merwe
Ministry of Environment and Tourism
National Archives of Namibia
South African Military Archive, Pretoria
The Scientific Society of Swakopmund
Namibia Scientific Society, Windhoek
Museum Afrika, Johannesburg
Western Cape Provincial Archives and Record Services
South African Railways and all the unknown personnel stationed at Garub over the years

**Gratitude is also due to the many concerned individuals
for their ongoing support for the Wild Horses in the Namib Desert.**

PHOTO CREDITS

Christine Swiegers
Gondwana photo library
Jan Coetzer
Martin Unger
Telané Greyling
Jaco Visser

Emil Kreplin album
HO Reuter
Judy & Scott Hurd
Piet Swiegers
Walter Rusch
FJ van der Merwe

Jean-Claude Herman
Helmut Schäfer
Mannfred Goldbeck
Ron Swilling
Willem Swiegers
Nampost Namibia

REFERENCES

- **AFRIKA**, Dr Phil Leonhard Scheben, Urban & Schwarzenberg, 1926
- **Boerperd: Die Geskiedenis van die SA Boerperd**, Kobus du Toit, West Publishers, 2005
- **Correspondence between CDM and SAR from 1977** re: the continuation of water at Garub for the horses, courtesy of Jan Coetzer
- **Der Feldzug in Südwest 1914/15**, Dr Hans von Oelhafen, Safari-Verlag, 1923
- **Desert Horses in Danger**, August Sycholt, Farmers Weekly, Nov 6 1992
- **Diamanten im Sand**, Olga Levinson, Kuiseb Publishers, 2007
- **Expelled from a Beloved Country**, Sven-Eric Kanzler, Nature Investments Pty Ltd, 2003
- **Factors Affecting Possible Management Strategies for the Namib Feral Horses**, T Greyling, 2005
- **How Botha and Smuts Conquered German South West**, Reuter's War Correspondents with the Forces, WS Rayner and WW O'Shaughnessy, Simpkin, Marshall, Hamilton, Kent & Co, 1916
- **Kreplin's guestbook and farewell letter to his daughter Fritzi**, courtesy of the Kreplin estate
- **Light Horse Cavalcade: The Imperial Light Horse 1899-1961**, Harry Klein, Howard Timmins, 1969
- **Lüderitzbuchter Zeitung**, 14 May 1910, 22 May 1910, 6 April 1920, 23 February 1925
- **Namibia-The Bradt Travel Guide**, Chris McIntyre, Bradt Publications, 2003
- **Notes on a Herd of Wild Horses in the Namib Desert 1984**, FJ van der Merwe, the Department of Agriculture South Africa, 1984
- **Riding High - Horses, Power and Settler Society c.1654-1840**, Kronos, vol29, Environmental History, Special Issue, Nov 2003
- **Riding in South West Africa-Today and Yesterday**, G Voigts and EJ Holtz
- **Southern and Central Namibia in Jonker Afrikaner's Time**, Brigitte Lau, Windhoek Archives Publication, 1987
- **Swakopmunder Zeitung**, 9 April 1932
- **The Campaign in German South West Africa 1914-1915**, Brigadier-General JJ Collyer, the Government Printer, 1937
- **The Cape Horse: Its Origin, Breeding and Development in the Union of South Africa**, Pieter Juriaan van der Heyde Schreuder, 1915
- **The Encyclopaedia of the Horse**, Elwyn Hartley Edwards, Dorling Kindersley, 1994.
- **The Firing Line, The Nongqai, 1914-15, the South-West African Campaign**, pg10
- **The First 100 years of State Railways in Namibia 1897-1997**, Brenda Bravenboer and Walter Rusch, TransNamib Museum, Windhoek, Namibia, 1997

- **The Nature of Horses: Their Evolution, Intelligence and Behaviour**, Stephen Budiansky, Phoenix, 1997
- **The Real Namib Desert Horses**, FJ van der Merwe, 2001
- **Treasures of the Diamond Coast: A Century of Diamond Mining in Namibia**, Gabi Schneider, Macmillan Education Namibia, 2008
- **Urgent Imperial Service: South African Forces in German South West Africa 1914-1915**, Gerald L'ange, Ashanti Publishing, 1991
- **Walter Rusch collection**
- **Wild Horses of the World**, Moira C. Harris, Hamlyn, 2009
- **Zucht und Remontirung der Militärpferde aller Staaten**, Dr Paul Goldbeck, Mittler und Sohn, 1901

'The ground trembled, gravel flew, dust rose.
Twelve horses galloped past me, so close I could smell their
wildness and feel the presence of a
boundless freedom.'

August Sycholt

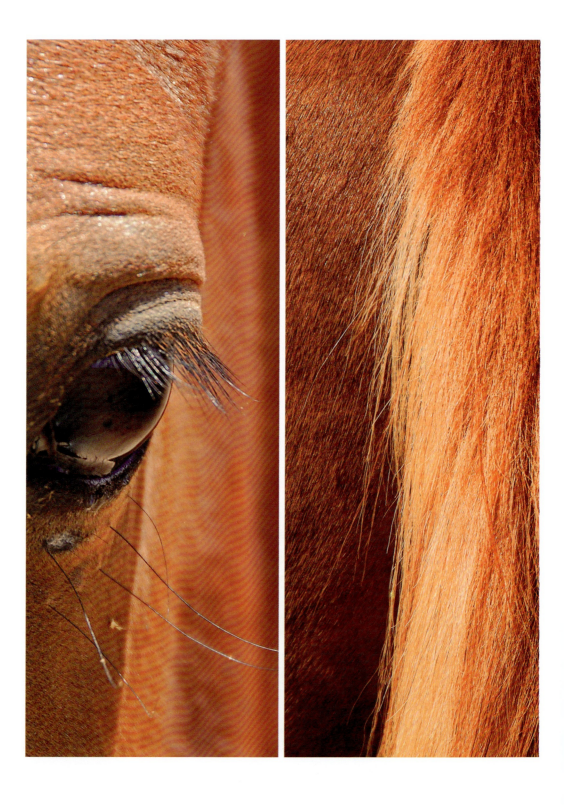